W9-AES-541

Florence Nightingale

A Photo-Illustrated Biography
by Lucile Davis

Consultant:
Byron Hyde, M.D.
Chairman
The Nightingale Research Foundation

Bridgestone Books

an imprint of Capstone Press
Mankato, Minnesota

Bridgestone Books are published by Capstone Press
818 North Willow Street, Mankato, Minnesota 56001
http://www.capstone-press.com

Library of Congress Cataloging-in-Publication Data
Davis, Lucile.
   Florence Nightingale: a photo-illustrated biography/by Lucile Davis.
   p. cm.—(Photo-illustrated biographies)
   Includes bibliographical references and index.
   Summary: A biography of the nurse and women's rights advocate who spent her life trying
to improve medical standards.
   ISBN 0-7368-0205-3
   1. Nightingale, Florence, 1820–1910—Juvenile literature. 2. Nurses—England—Biography—
Juvenile literature. [1. Nightingale, Florence, 1820–1910. 2. Nurses. 3. Women—Biography]
I. Title. II. Series.
RT37.N5D38 1999
610.73'092—dc21
[B]
                                                                           98-46009
                                                                                CIP
                                                                                AC

Editorial Credits
Chuck Miller, editor; Timothy Halldin, cover designer and illustrator; Kimberly Danger, photo
   researcher

Photo Credits
Archive Photos, cover, 8, 12, 14; Kean Archives, 4; Popperfoto, 16
Corbis/Hulton-Deutsch Collection, 20
Corbis-Bettmann, 6
National Institutes of Health/Corbis, 18

Table of Contents

Founder of Modern Nursing

Florence Nightingale is the founder of modern nursing. A nurse's duties once were much like a maid's duties. But Florence changed that. She believed nurses should have special training to learn how to care for patients. Florence helped start a nursing school and wrote many books about nursing. Florence made nursing a respected profession.

Florence believed that God had asked for her help. But she was not sure what God wanted her to do. Florence took an interest in nursing at age 17. She thought nursing must be what God wanted her to do.

Florence became interested in nursing against her family's wishes. Her parents did not consider nursing a respectable job. But Florence earned the respect of people in England and around the world. Florence became famous for her service during the Crimean War (1853–1856).

Florence made nursing a respectable job. People around the world honored her for her service during the Crimean War.

Childhood in England

Florence Nightingale was born in Florence, Italy, on May 12, 1820. Her family was from England. They were on vacation in Italy when Florence was born. Her parents decided to name her after the Italian city.

Florence's mother was Frances Smith Nightingale. Florence's father was William Edward Nightingale. The Nightingale family was wealthy. William was well educated. He had studied at Cambridge University in England.

William taught Florence and her older sister, Parthenope (PAR-then-O-pee), at home. They studied history and math. William also taught Florence and her sister to speak many languages. Florence enjoyed her studies. She was a good student. Florence's favorite subject was math.

It was unusual for a young woman to receive an education in the 1800s. But Florence enjoyed her studies and was a good student.

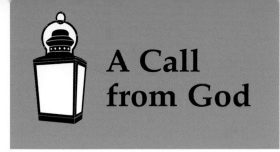

A Call from God

Florence believed she received a call from God on February 7, 1837. She believed God wanted her to live a life of service. But Florence did not know what kind of service God wanted her to do.

Florence liked to care for people who were sick. She visited hospitals when her family traveled to other countries. Florence wanted to know how to take better care of people who were sick.

In 1850, Florence visited a hospital in Kaiserwerth (KYE-zur-wurth), Germany. The hospital trained women to be nurses. After the visit, Florence realized that God wanted her to be a nurse.

In 1851, Florence trained to be a nurse at the hospital in Kaiserwerth. Florence finished her training in three months. She soon was in charge of a women's hospital in London.

Florence believed that God wanted her to be a nurse.

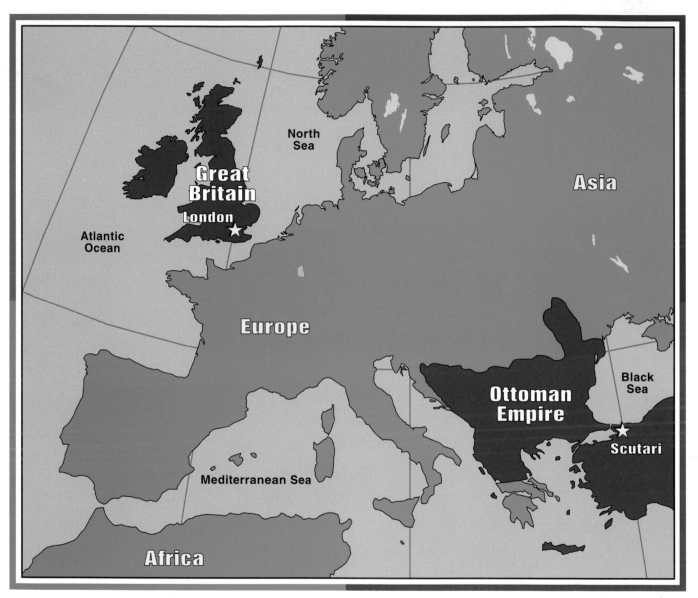

Great Britain and the Ottoman Empire During the Crimean War (1853–1856)

The Crimean War

In 1854, England and France declared war on Russia. The Crimean War was fought for control of the Ottoman Empire. Part of this area of land is now Turkey. Russia wanted to divide the Ottoman Empire and take part of it. England and France wanted the Ottoman Empire to stay together.

Many British soldiers were hurt in the Crimean War. The British army did not have nurses. England's minister of war, Sidney Herbert, heard that Florence was trained in nursing. He asked her to bring nurses to a British army hospital.

In 1854, Florence and 38 nurses traveled to Scutari. This city was in the Ottoman Empire. Florence and the other nurses did more than treat the soldiers' wounds. The nurses helped the soldiers write letters and send money home. Florence set up classrooms for the soldiers in the hospital.

England was far away from the Ottoman Empire. Florence helped British soldiers write letters and send money home.

"I stand at the altar of murdered men, and, while I live, I fight their cause."
—Florence in a letter to a friend in 1856

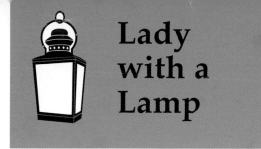

Lady with a Lamp

The Crimean War ended in 1856 when Russian officials signed a peace agreement. They agreed to remove Russia's army from the Ottoman Empire.

Florence and other nurses had won the respect of British soldiers during the war. Florence was called the "lady with a lamp" in a poem by Henry Wadsworth Longfellow. Florence was known for walking the hospital hallways with a lamp each night. She offered care to anyone who needed it.

Florence was concerned about British army hospitals. The hospitals were not sanitary. They were dirty and full of germs. Germs can cause infections. More soldiers died from infections than from wounds during the Crimean War.

Florence had worked to make army hospitals in the Ottoman Empire sanitary. But she also knew she had to help improve army hospitals in England.

Florence stayed up late at night to care for soldiers.

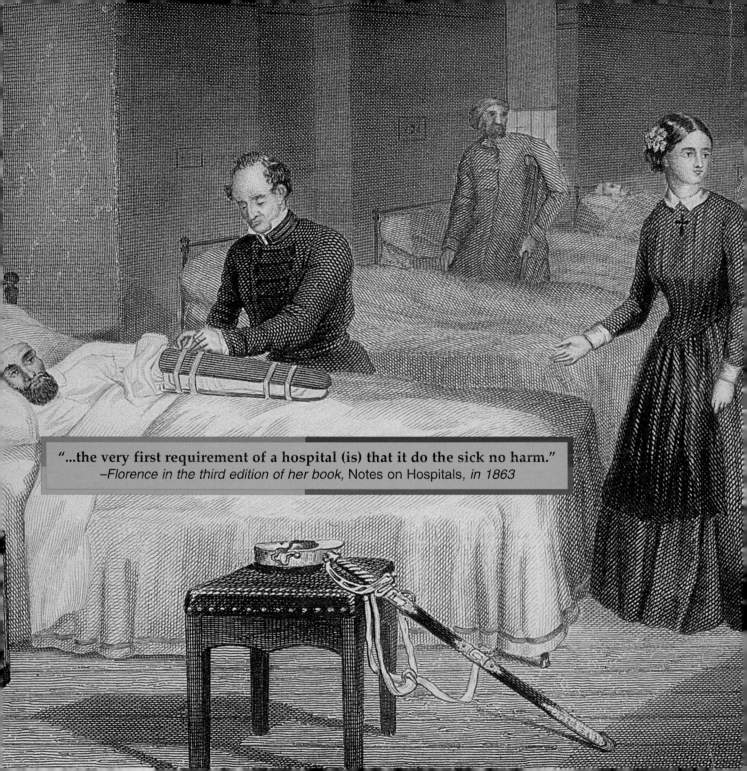

"...the very first requirement of a hospital (is) that it do the sick no harm."
–*Florence in the third edition of her book,* Notes on Hospitals, *in 1863*

Making Hospitals Sanitary

Florence met England's Queen Victoria in 1856. She told the queen about unsanitary conditions in British army hospitals. Florence suggested the queen form a royal commission. This group of British officials would decide how to improve army hospitals.

Queen Victoria asked Sidney Herbert to lead the commission. Florence wrote reports about the dirty conditions in army hospitals. She presented the reports to the commission.

Florence's efforts led the commission to create an army medical school in 1860. Army hospitals improved as a result. England then had the most sanitary army hospitals of any country in Europe.

Florence published two important medical books in 1860. *Notes on Hospitals* is about building sanitary hospitals. *Notes on Nursing* explains diseases and proper nursing care.

British army hospitals improved because of Florence. England then had the most sanitary hospitals of any country in Europe.

Training Others

Florence believed nurses needed better training to work in hospitals. In 1860, she helped start the Nightingale Training School. This nursing school was at St. Thomas Hospital in London.

Nursing students at the Nightingale school trained for one year. They took some classes. But they mostly worked in the hospital.

The school's students learned how to help doctors treat patients. They also learned Florence's ways of keeping hospitals clean. Florence made the nursing students write reports of their daily activities. She carefully read over the reports herself.

Florence cared about her students. She invited the school's graduates to her home. Florence had tea with them. She also gave them nursing books. The graduates traveled to hospitals in England and other countries to train others.

Florence invited students to her home when they graduated. The new nurses would train others as Florence had trained them.

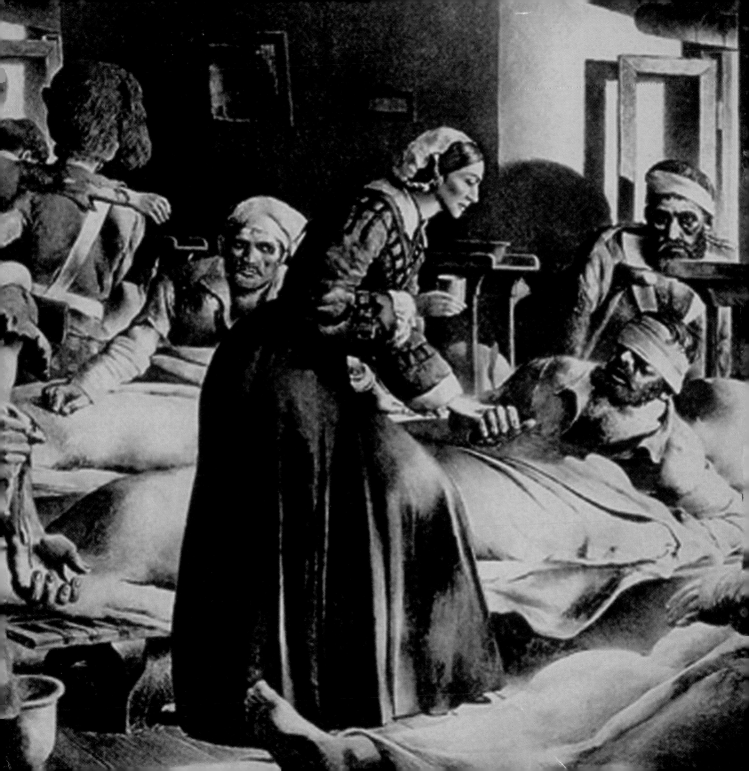

Health Care Adviser

In 1861, Florence became very sick. She stayed in bed at her home in London.

Many people believe Florence had chronic fatigue syndrome. This disease makes people very tired. They are so weak that they often cannot get out of bed. An infection or stress can cause chronic fatigue syndrome. Florence had worked long hours and treated many infections during the Crimean War.

But Florence kept working from her bed. She improved British government hospitals. Florence worked to make conditions more sanitary in the government hospitals.

Florence also worked to improve medical conditions in India. This country was an English colony. Florence wrote a report about health care in India. Her report led to better health care in India.

Florence's experiences during the Crimean War probably led her to develop chronic fatigue syndrome.

Later Years

Other people noticed Florence's work as a health care adviser. In 1861, the U.S. Army asked for Florence's advice. The U.S. Army used her ideas to set up army hospitals during the U.S. Civil War (1861–1865).

Florence helped start the British Red Cross in 1870. This group helps victims of disasters such as wars or floods.

Florence continued to write about health care from her bed. She published 200 books, reports, and articles about improving medical standards.

In 1907, Florence became the first woman to receive the British Order of Merit. Florence received the award for helping improve England's health care system.

Florence died in her home on August 13, 1910, at the age of 90. Her efforts inspired health care improvements still in place today.

Florence improved health care around the world. She did this even though she could not get out of bed for much of her life.

Fast Facts about Florence Nightingale

 Florence learned to speak Greek and Latin as a young girl.

 Florence often worked 16 to 24 hours a day as a nurse during the Crimean War.

 Florence gave medical advice to the U.S. Army during the Civil War. This advice saved the lives of thousands of U.S. soldiers.

Dates in Florence Nightingale's Life

1820—Born May 12 in Florence, Italy

1837—Believes she receives a call from God on February 7

1851—Attends nurse training hospital in Kaiserwerth, Germany

1854—Helps care for British soldiers during the Crimean War

1856—Helps form a British royal commission on army hospitals

1860—Founds the Nightingale Training School for nurses

1860—Publishes *Notes on Hospitals* and *Notes on Nursing*

1861—Advises the U.S. Army about military hospitals

1870—Helps start the British Red Cross

1907—Awarded the British Order of Merit by King Edward VII

1910—Dies August 13 in London

Words to Know

Crimean War (krye-MEE-an WOR)—a war in which England and France stopped Russia from taking part of the Ottoman Empire; part of this area of land is now Turkey.

empire (EM-pyre)—a group of countries that have the same ruler

germ (JUHRM)—a living cell that can cause a disease or illness

graduate (GRAJ-oo-it)—someone who has finished all the required classes at a school

infection (in-FEK-shuhn)—an illness caused by germs; chronic fatigue syndrome can be caused by an infection or too much stress.

profession (pruh-FESH-uhn)—a job that requires special training; Florence made nursing a profession.

sanitary (SAN-uh-ter-ee)—clean and free from germs

Read More

Colver, Anne. *Florence Nightingale, War Nurse.* A Discovery Biography. New York: Chelsea Juniors, 1992.

Mosher, Kiki. *Learning about Compassion from the Life of Florence Nightingale.* A Character Building Book. New York: Rosen/PowerKids Press, 1996.

Shor, Donnali. *Florence Nightingale.* What Made Them Great. Englewood Cliffs, N.J.: Silver Burdett Press, 1990.

Useful Addresses

The Florence Nightingale Foundation
1 Grosvenor Crescent
London SW1X 7EE
United Kingdom

The Florence Nightingale Museum
2 Lambeth Palace Road
London SE1 7EW
United Kingdom

Internet Sites

Florence Nightingale
http://gnv.fdt.net/~dforest/fnindex.htm
Florence Nightingale Museum
http://www.florence-nightingale.co.uk
Lady with the Lamp–Florence Nightingale
http://nursing.miningco.com/library/weekly/aa051498.htm

Index

AAV- 6764